D0931565

MY FIRST LOOK AT INSECTS

BUTTERFLIES ARE AMAZING INSECTS

# Butterflies

TERESA WIMMER

Marysville Public Library
231 S. Plum St.
Marysville, OH 43040
(937) 642-1876

CREATIVE EDUCATION

Published by Creative Education

123 South Broad Street, Mankato, Minnesota 56001

Creative Education is an imprint of The Creative Company

Designed by Rita Marshall

Photographs by Getty Images (Jonathan Blair, Gay Bumgarner, George Grall, Darrell Gulin, Margarette Mead, Ryan / Beyer, Kevin Schafer, Stephen Sharnoff)

Copyright © 2007 Creative Education

International copyright reserved in all countries. No part of this book may be reproduced in any form without written permission from the publisher.

Printed in the United States of America

**Library of Congress Cataloging-in-Publication Data**

Wimmer, Teresa. Butterflies / by Teresa Wimmer.

p. cm. – (My first look at: insects)

Includes index.

ISBN-13 : 978-1-58341-455-2

1. Butterflies—Juvenile literature. I. Title

QL544.2.W54 2006       595.78'9—dc22       2005037238

First edition  9 8 7 6 5 4 3 2 1

# Butterflies

## Coat of Colors

Look outside in the spring and summer. You might see a butterfly flying around. Butterflies are pretty **insects**. They have two wings on each side of their body.

Butterfly wings come in many colors. Some butterflies have blue, red, or yellow wings. Others have green or brown wings.

**SOME BUTTERFLIES' WINGS LOOK SHINY**

Butterflies have two eyes. Their eyes help them watch out for enemies such as birds, spiders, and other insects.

Butterflies do not have a nose. Instead, they have two **antennae** on the top of their head. Butterflies use their antennae to smell and find food. Their antennae help them feel things, too. When butterflies fly, their antennae help them feel the wind.

Butterflies have hairs on
their feet. The hairs help them
taste flowers and find food.

A CLOSE-UP VIEW OF A BUTTERFLY'S BODY

## A Big World

Butterflies live in most places on Earth. Some live in woods or fields. Others live on mountains. Some butterflies live in hot, dry places called deserts.

Most butterflies fly alone during the day. When it rains, they take cover in trees, bushes, or tall weeds. At night, some butterflies gather in small groups. They sleep in the grass or under leaves.

Butterfly wings are very thin.

When butterflies get older,

pieces of their wings break off.

Most butterflies do not like cold weather. During the winter, some butterflies **migrate** to stay warm. Monarch butterflies fly to trees far away from their home. They find the same trees every year.

## FROM CATERPILLAR TO BUTTERFLY

A butterfly does not have wings when it is born. It starts out as a caterpillar. Caterpillars look like worms with many legs. They are green or brown. Some caterpillars are furry. Others are smooth.

A GROUP OF MIGRATING MONARCH BUTTERFLIES

A caterpillar eats a lot of leaves. It grows bigger and bigger. After a few weeks, the caterpillar crawls onto a leaf. It hangs upside down from the leaf.

Then it spins a hard shell around its body. The hard shell is called a chrysalis (*KRISS–uh–liss*). Inside the chrysalis, the caterpillar turns into a butterfly! The butterfly does not grow any bigger.

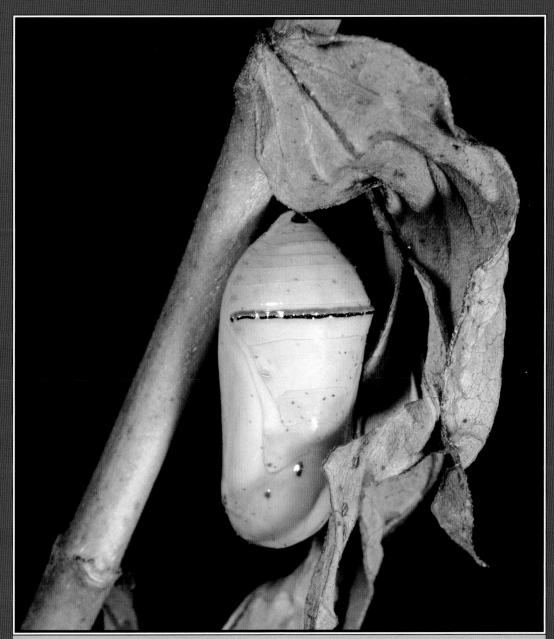

**A CHRYSALIS HANGING FROM A BRANCH**

## Butterflies and Flowers

Butterflies get their food from flowers. Flowers make **nectar** in their stems. Butterflies sip the nectar. Their mouth is shaped like a straw. They suck the nectar through the straw.

When butterflies land on flowers, **pollen** sticks to their feet. They carry the pollen from flower to flower. The pollen helps the flowers grow.

Caterpillars are picky
eaters. They will eat only
certain kinds of plants.

A BUTTERFLY SIPPING NECTAR FROM A FLOWER

BUTTERFLIES AND FLOWERS NEED EACH OTHER

Some people plant "butterfly gardens." These are gardens full of flowers that butterflies like. People plant pink, yellow, red, and purple flowers in butterfly gardens. Then they watch the butterflies fly from flower to flower!

A butterfly cannot fly if
it is cold. It has to stand
in the sun to warm up.

BUTTERFLIES LIKE BRIGHT-COLORED FLOWERS

# Hands-on: Make a Caterpillar Home

Caterpillars grow into pretty butterflies. You can catch a caterpillar in the spring and watch it change.

## What You Need

A glass jar with holes
      poked in the lid
A small twig

A handful of leaves
A handful of dirt

## What You Do

1. Put the twig, leaves, and dirt in the glass jar.
2. Look for a caterpillar on a plant or on the ground. Put it in the jar.
3. Put the lid on the jar.
4. Make sure the caterpillar always has enough leaves to eat.
5. When your caterpillar turns into a butterfly, look at its pretty colors. Then, take the jar outside. Watch your butterfly fly away!

THIS CATERPILLAR WILL TURN INTO A BUTTERFLY

## Index

## Words to Know

**antennae**—long rods used by butterflies for smelling and feeling

**insects**—small animals that have six legs

**migrate**—move from one place to another, usually to find warmth or food

**nectar**—a sweet juice that flowers make

**pollen**—a yellow powder that flowers make

## Read More

Brimner, Larry Dane. *Butterflies and Moths.* New York: Grolier Children's Press, 1999.

Norsgaard, E. Jaediker. *Butterflies for Kids.* Minnetonka, Minn.: NorthWord Press, 1996.

Rockwell, Anne. *Becoming Butterflies.* New York: Walker and Company, 2002.

## Explore the Web

**AllAboutButterflies.com** http://www.enchantedlearning.com/subjects/butterfly

**Foremost's Butterflies Are Blooming** http://www.foremostbutterflies.com

**NBII Children's Butterfly Site** http://mpin.nbii.gov/insects/kidsbutterfly/
index.html